Be Your Own Dream Detective

How to Interpret ANY Dream

by The Dream Guy

AN

PROJECT

Published by nhBeyond 2024

A CIP catalogue for this book is available from the British Library.

Paperback ISBN

ACKNOWLEDGEMENTS

I would like to thank all of those people who came to me for help interpreting their dreams. Without your raw data, I wouldn't have been able to refine the LIF® interpretation system.

Thanks also to Jane and the children for often being my sounding board when it comes to the understanding of dreams.

CHAPTER 1

A ROYAL ROAD

Freud once referred to dream interpretation as the "royal road to a knowledge of the unconscious," and though many scientists, occultists, mystics and artists have since added their voices to this fascinating subject matter, that one phrase still rings true. Of course, dream interpretation had been going on for a long time before Freud and the subject of dreams has been explored from a multitude of angles before and since his work. Some rationalists dismiss dreams as the meaningless ramblings of a tired brain; psychologists and psychiatrists have explained them in terms of repressed wishes or archetypal patterns and religious mystics have revered them as visions sent by God. Who is right?

During my dream consultations I have found the explanations of Swiss psychiatrist Carl Gustav Jung to most closely match what I have discovered. Jung suggested that dreams were communications from the unconscious and had their own purpose and language. As my own experience accumulated, both from interpreting my own dreams and those of my clients, I became increasingly aware of the incredible subtlety and wisdom encoded within them. I couldn't believe these messages arrived as a result of some sort of random brain chatter and I referred to their origin as the 'Dream Source,' because I didn't want to jump to any conclusions and this seemed like the safest term to use. I have stuck with it ever since.

Other people and organisations have cast further light into the hidden depths of the realm of dreams, voices from sources as diverse as the Theosophical Society, ancient shamanic cultures, modern laboratory-based dream research and, of course, personal anecdotes from those I have worked and lived with.

Before I move on to explain the development of my own interpretation framework I will present a short history of dream interpretation in the 'west,' a journey which leads from the temples of ancient Egypt and Greece, through the clinics of Freud and Jung and on to the laboratories and institutes of modern dream researchers.

CHAPTER 2

FROM EGYPT TO CHICAGO

The Ancient Egyptians

One of the earliest pieces of evidence proving that dream interpretation was practised in Ancient times, comes from a dream book found in the library of Egyptian scribe Kenhirkhopeshef. This library, discovered in the city of Deir el-Medina, dates from at least 1527 to 1506 B.C., although the dream book is said to have been old even then! Dreams were interpreted by priests or qualified interpreters (an honour conferred only by the gods) and were seen as divine omens. Dream symbols were categorised as 'good' or 'bad', as the following examples illustrate:

- To dream of eating crocodile flesh means you will become a village official.
- Plunging into cold waters means you will be absolved of all ills.
- Making love to your wife in daylight shows that your god will discover your misdeeds.

The Ancient Greeks

The cult of Asclepius, god of healing and medicine, sprang up in around 300 B.C., and temples known as Asclepeions were erected throughout Greece. In an example of what is now known as 'dream incubation' the sick and injured would sleep overnight at the temples in order to inspire dreaming. Sometimes they were even surrounded by non-venomous snakes since these were sacred to Asclepius. In the morning the patients would report their dreams to the priest who would then interpret them and prescribe a cure.

Biblical Dreams

The Bible is full of references to visions and dreams, believed to be important vehicles for divine revelation. The most famous dream interpreter in the Bible is of course Joseph, son of Jacob, whose interpretative skills led toboth trouble and triumph (see below). Another well-known Biblical dreamer was Daniel, who interpreted the dreams of the ruler of Babylon, King Nebuchadnezzar.

Famous Dream #1:

Joseph and the 7 Fat and 7 Lean Kine

While imprisoned in the house of Potiphar, Joseph interpreted the dreams of two of his fellow inmates: the Pharaoh's chief butler and chief baker. He predicted that the baker would be executed but the butler reinstated, asking the butler to plead his case to the Pharaoh when the time came. However, the butler forgot his oath. That is, until the Pharaoh revealed he had been troubled by a dream in which seven lean kine devoured seven fat kine and seven withered ears of corn devoured seven full, ripe ones. The butler told the Pharaoh of Joseph's skill and Joseph was sent for. He interpreted the dream as referring to seven years of famine that were to follow seven years of

abundance, recommending that an able appointee should be charged with storing grain. Delighted with this interpretation, the Pharaoh appointed Joseph viceroy of Egypt.

The Work of Sigmund Freud

To many, especially those familiar with psychology, dream interpretation is synonymous with one famous figure: Austrian psychologist Sigmund Freud. His 1900 publication, 'The Interpretation of Dreams' set out Freud's early thoughts on this subject. This book was written before Freud had established his famous drive/structure model and dreams were explained as a compromise between 'wish-fulfilment,' the dreamer's instinctive desire to re-experience previous (often erotic) pleasures, and the regulations imposed by society, internalised as a 'censor' (probably a pre-cursor to the notion of the structure ego).

Freud also explained that the source of the hidden (which he termed 'latent') dream could be found in the previous day's preoccupations. The experienced (manifest) dream was not to be taken seriously in itself and the able interpreter (i.e. a psychoanalyst) would use it merely to decode the dream symbols. The censor would use a number of ploys to disguise the latent dream including condensation (where one symbol stands for a combination of ideas) and displacement (where threatening impulses are offloaded onto non-threatening symbols). In addition, the censor reworked the dream into an acceptable form in a process named secondary elaboration. Freud explained the occurrence of disturbing nightmares as examples of when the censorship process had failed although he admitted that the replaying of traumatic experiences in dreams was an exception for which he had no answer.

<u>Famous Dream #2</u>:

Irma's Injection

In 'The Interpretation of Dreams,' Freud turned his interpretative skills on to himself by analysing his own dream involving a patient called Irma. In the dream, Irma is unwell with stomach and throat problems. Freud initially blames Irma for not following his recommendations but later, after consulting with his medical colleagues (an unusual looking Dr. M. and Otto), he suspects Otto of negligence with a contaminated needle. He also saw the chemical formula for trimethylamin in his dream, a chemical he was studying in relation to sexual processes. The formula was printed in heavy type. After free association on the previous day's events he interpreted the dream as involving his wish to offload responsibility for Irma's problems and also his sexual feelings for her. He also related the accusations of negligence not to Otto but to his best friend Fleiss who had been negligent by leaving plasters in the nasal cavity of another of Freud's patients. To Freud, this was an example of the displacement of his anger.

The Work of Carl Gustav Jung

Carl Gustav Jung (1875-1961) was a Swiss psychiatrist who drew from a range of scientific, literary and philosophical sources in his exploration of the human psyche. He placed great value on the search and achievement of psychological integration and founded the discipline of analytical psychology. Regarding the interpretation of dreams, Jung regarded Freud's theories as incomplete.

Although he agreed that the raw material of the manifest dream could be causally related to previous experiences, he argued that dream states, in accordance with all psychic structures, had 'some sense of purpose inherent in them' (p.27). For example, in 'Dreams,' (pp 31-33), he reveals the case of a client who had been having an affair and had experienced a dream whereby he was eating an apple and feeling guilty. A Freudian analyst would have little problem interpreting this dream: the apple-eating was both the wish-fulfilment and its repression by the censor (which replaced the sexual act with a more acceptable symbolic replacement). Jung's dissatisfaction with such an explanation lay in the particular symbol 'chosen,' a motif intimately associated with issues of temptation, betrayal, morality and judgment. Jung saw a purpose in this man's dream: to force him to confront a moral issue he had so far failed to consider in his waking life. From his considerable empirical experience, Jung was convinced that dreams often provided this kind of compensatory reaction to unbalanced psychological states.

To Jung, dreams reflected the richness and complexity of the personal and collective unconscious of which Freud's forbidden desires were just a part (albeit a powerful part he termed the 'shadow' archetype). The existence of the collective unconscious and the archetypes are among Jung's most valuable contributions to dream interpretation.

The collective unconscious has been described as a repository of all the experiences of our species, a reservoir of dream symbols which can and do arise in dreams from across cultures and times. The extent to whether Jung conceptualised this repository in mystical terms (i.e. a group soul) is debatable. His initial definition was certainly presented in a more biological light but during the course of his work, Jung clearly moved towards a more spiritual perspective on life. The archetypes were key patterns within the collective unconscious and exhibited autonomy within the psyche so that they became real entities to those who encountered them in dreams.

Since the benefit of holistic integration was a key element of Jung's theory, meeting and understanding unconscious attitudes in the form of the archetypes was seen as healing. Jung saw the psyche as self-regulating, compensating for unbalanced conscious attitudes with their opposites within dreams. Unlike Freud, Jung placed importance on interpreting the manifest dream which stemmed from the unconscious and hence contained its own primacy and logic, communicated through dynamic symbols. Jung also saw dream interpretation as involving both analyst and client since an intimate knowledge of a client's personal situation was necessary. He also admitted the existence of philosophical truths and telepathic communications within dreams, prompting Freud to eventually dismiss his former correspondent as a 'prophet'.

From 1950 to Today: Modern Dream Research

The study of dreams is known as oneirology, a term originating in the 17th century, but it took until the mid 20th century for psychologists to take dreams away from the psychotherapist's clinic and submit them to scientific scrutiny. In 1953, experimental psychologist Calvin S. Hall Jr presented his cognitive theory of dreams, based on a huge body of dream reports, from which he deduced that dreaming involves the creation of numerous internal symbols to represent the dreamer's own personal conceptions. These symbols could also be seen in poetry and slang.

At around the same time, Professor Nathaniel Kleitman and his student Eugene Aserinsky discovered sleep cycles and four years later, Kleitman and another student, William C. Dement related the REM stage to dreaming. Today, dream research continues on a number of psychological fronts using the latest brain imaging and computer modelling techniques. At the time of writing numerous studies are ongoing. For example, recent studies have been published on how dreams relate to the process of memory consolidation, how nightmares are experienced in non-western cultures, the effects of noise on REM sleep and dream recall and possible interactions between the Earth's magnetic field and melatonin as a hypothesis for bizarre dream formation.

Before moving on to the exciting part I would like to introduce myself briefly and give you some insight into my own journey into the fascinating realm of dreams.

CHAPTER 3

MY STORY

Monroe's OOBE

When writing this book, I endeavoured to retrace my steps to uncover exactly why I became interested in dream interpretation. For a start, I grew up in Cornwall, a mystical county full of strange tales and happenings. My family were generally interested and open-minded on issues of religion and belief. However, if my particular fascination with dreams and states of consciousness in general had a starting point, I would have to mention Robert Monroe and his book, 'Journeys Out of the Body.'

'Bob' Monroe (1915-1995) was the president of multi-million dollar corporation, a businessman with a self-proclaimed good scientific and medical background. One spring Sunday afternoon in 1958, he had been listening to a tape designed to aid dream recall and suffered an 'iron-hard cramp' beneath his rib cage over the solar plexus area. The discomfort lasted until after midnight when he eventually fell asleep. Three weeks later and on numerous occasions over a six week period, he would be lying down when a 'warm light' would strike him, paralysing him and causing his body to vibrate. His doctor could find no physical abnormalities so Monroe began to pay close attention to his experiences to try and work out what was going on.

The vibrations would be accompanied by a roaring sound as they passed from his toes to his head at a rate of five cycles a second. He was also aware of a ring of blue sparks, two feet in diameter. Several months later, late at night, he was trying to sleep and felt the familiar vibrations again. At the time he was idly touching a rug on the floor but as he pushed down, his hand went straight through the rug, the floor and the ceiling. He felt a chip of wood, a bent nail and only when he rested his hand in a pool of water did he realise he was having a very strange experience. Four weeks later, he awoke from a daydream to find himself brushing against the ceiling. On looking down at his bed he saw his wife with another man – of course the other man was himself. Monroe, unsurprisingly, describes such Out of Body Experiences (OOBEs) as 'one of the most profound experiences of a person's life' and in 1972 he founded the Monroe Institute of Applied Sciences (existing today as the Monroe Institute).

My OOBE

In the late nineties, I read Monroe's book which is remarkable in that it actually contains the precise visualisation techniques he himself used when inducing OOBE's. I decided to follow these visualisation techniques and, to my surprise, after a few attempts I too felt Monroe's vibrations. I then went on to experience vague sensations of floating and sensory 'hallucinations,' which I interpret as semi-OOBEs. Then, one moonlit night, I again practised the technique while lying down to sleep. As I slipped out of consciousness, I felt the vibrations again. This time when

I awoke, I was upright and floating in the air, having my first experience of an OOBE.

Although this book only touches on OOBEs and lucid dreaming, this was certainly the most profound moment of my life and the event which launched me on a voyage of discovery into dreams and altered states of consciousness.

On the Shaman's Path

At this time I became interested in shamanism after discovering how the shaman's perspective on dreaming was remarkably different to that of the West and more in keeping with the experiences of Monroe and myself. Shamanic practices predate and to a large extent underlie most, if not all, of the organised forms of religion in existence today. One common element of shamanic practice involves the 'shamanic journey.' This is a method by which shaman's move from ordinary reality to an equally real 'non-ordinary' reality in order to contact spiritual forces for advice and assistance. Shamans also often play the role of 'psychopomp,' a guide for spirits of the deceased who have become lost.

Although shamanism often brings to mind the 'medicine men' of the native Americans or the 'witch-doctor' of Africa, there are shamanic traditions from all over the world, including traditional witchcraft here in the UK. Although there are practitioners within these traditions today, shamanism can be practised in a modern context, without the need to adopt ancient customs that may seem contrived.

Such 'core shamanic' practices have become popular due largely to the work of Michael Harner, author of the classic book, 'Way of the Shaman.' I read widely on shamanism and all approaches seemed to have a few things in common when discussing dreams: they were not to be ignored, they had potentially healing and philosophical benefits and the figures within them were real entities who, when contacted and understood, could become allies. But did anyone in the annals of modern dream research corroborate these ancient beliefs? It was then that I came across Jung from an unlikely source: the popular writings of Pamela Ball.

Back to Jung

Pamela Ball's ***10,000 Dreams Interpreted*** (now republished as the ***Quantum Dream Dictionary***) is surely one of the most comprehensive dream dictionaries available on the market. It is grounded in the work of Jung and explains in depth about the Jungian archetypes and how they manifest themselves in dreams. With this theoretical grounding, I set to work interpreting my own dreams and those of my friends.

As suggested by Ball, I 'incubated' my dreams by setting my alarm and noting down the results in my journal and I soon became convinced of the power and subtlety contained in the dream messages. However, I often came across two stumbling blocks, really two sides of one paradoxical coin.

One side harks back to the theories of Freud. It seemed that some people were determined to stick with an 'acceptable' interpretation of their dream. Resistance is the psychodynamic term for this process and is what the psychoanalytic method itself was created to address (Jung 9). How could I create an interpretative method that could overcome such stubborn resistance to analysis?

The other side of the coin involved validation. How could I, with no subjective experience of another's dream, be sure I had come up with a valid interpretation. I addressed the first issue by creating a layered interpretative framework: a systematic process which was to be applied, in an invariable order, to all dreams.

Just as a good detective will not be deceived by the motives of biased witnesses, a good dream analyst, by rigorously following the framework, will not be swayed by the dreamer's – or his or her own – biased ego. The solution to my second dilemma came from one final influential book.

Bringing it Together

The missing piece came from a book by Eugene Gendlin. More commonly associated with the theory and techniques of focusing, Gendlin also wrote a book called 'Let Your Body Interpret Your Dreams' where he described the 'felt sense', a subtle 'knowingness' that can be felt physically in the body and becomes more accessible (yet no more definite) by awareness.

One sentence from Gendlin's book proved to be the key that enabled me to know whether my interpretations were on track or not. Gendlin writes:

'The felt sense will not resonate with a word or phrase that doesn't adequately 'say' it.'

In other words if an interpretation does not lead to an experience of 'rightness', felt somewhere in the client's own body, then the interpretation is either not valid or has not been communicated adequately. By incorporating Jungian symbolism and the felt sense into a central position in my layered interpretative framework (LIF) I created a powerful tool that has enabled me to interpret a wide array of dreams.

In fact, I believe that this framework can potentially interpret ANY dream.

CHAPTER 4

THE INTERPRETATIVE FRAMEWORK: AN OVERVIEW

Preparatory Notes

You may already work with your own dreams on a regular basis but if you don't and you are keen to start you will probably find it beneficial to begin 'incubating' dreams. The simplest method consists of two phases. The first part involves instructing yourself to remember your dreams as you fall to sleep each night. The more relaxed you are the better as the instruction is more likely to be received and acted upon by the subconscious mind. The second part requires you to keep a pad and pen by your bed (and ideally a source of adequate light) so that you can immediately jot down any details before they are lost.

<u>Famous Dream #3:</u>
Loewi and the Nervous System
A reminder of the importance of noting your dreams down legibly can be found in the dream experiences of Otto Loewi. A pharmacologist from Germany, Loewi was convinced that the nervous system transmitted messages by chemical means. The accepted knowledge of the time was that electrical transmission was sufficient to explain nervous transmission. It took Loewi many years to prove his theories (and later to win the Nobel Prize) and the vital experiment which proved his case came to him, on two consecutive nights, whilst he dreamed. On the first night he had written down the details but, to his horror, was unable to read his own handwriting in the morning. The second night he left nothing to chance, going straight to his laboratory upon waking to perform the crucial experiment.

Be patient as the process can take a while to start working, especially if this work is new to you. If you feel you are getting no results you might find it beneficial to write your instruction on a piece of paper and place it beneath your pillow. If you still feel you need assistance, crystals such as celestite, blue howlite, jasper and kyanite are said to be beneficial for aiding dream recall or you may find some of the herbal mixtures in New Age shops useful. The important thing is to experiment and be patient. At a certain point in your work it will seem as if the Dream Source itself starts to respond and your dreams should start becoming more vivid, more memorable and less mundane.

Using the Framework to Interpret Dreams

Jung suggested that analysing dreams required the, 'methodical questioning of [the] dreamer's associations.' (Jung 73) and that's one reason why I think a framework is necessary.

The following seven chapters take you step-by-step through the different elements of a dream. Some elements may not be present in some dreams or may not have been recalled. These elements can be skipped but be aware that the dreamer may suddenly remember forgotten parts of the dream as the interpretation progresses. The structural chart at the bottom of this page can be a useful reference aid to ensure every element of the dream is considered systematically.

Just as in a detective story, as you build your 'case' try to draw links between different parts of the dream to see if patterns emerge. If you are interpreting someone else's dream, present your evidence and watch for their reaction. Here is where the 'felt sense' comes in.

The Importance of Using the Felt Sense

As described earlier, Gendlin's 'felt sense' is a subtle physical sensation that occurs in the body when it reacts to truth. Although it is difficult to describe it is unmistakeable when you do experience it. The 'felt sense' is different to a purely academic certainty although it is usually accompanied by a sudden insight into your dream with several pieces just seeming to fall into place at once. Becoming aware of the physical sensation that accompanies this realisation is the key to using the 'felt sense' in all areas of your life.

Clearly, it is more difficult to judge somebody else's physical reaction to a valid interpretation but if you observe closely you will often find that the person's posture or attitude changes quite dramatically and they may start talking about life events they hadn't mentioned before.

A Visual Guide to the Layered Interpretative Framework®

Here is a link to the LIF® pictured below (if you are reading the Kindle version).

If you are reading the paperback or have any issues accessing the pdf please email me at beyond@nhbeyond.com

Use this framework to help with your own dream interpretations. For example, you can print it out and tick the boxes as you work through each area of interest, or you can create headings in a separate dream work book or on sheets of paper.

If you want to circulate this visual guide, please attribute to 'The Dream Guy' and provide a link where appropriate.

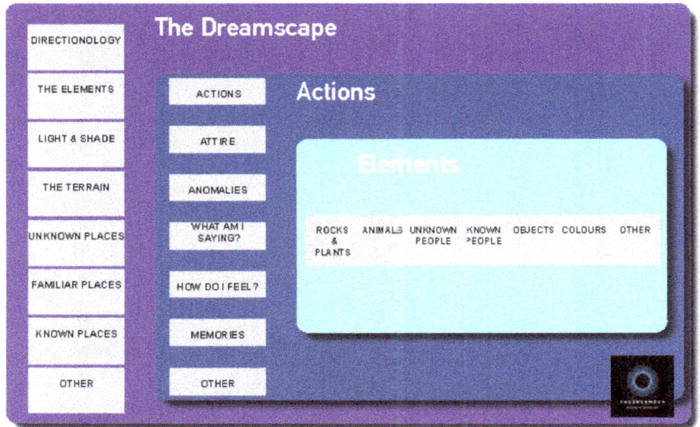

CHAPTER 5

EXPLORING THE DREAM LANDSCAPE

"A dream is a theatre in which the dreamer is himself the scene."
-Carl Gustav Jung-

Like Jung, the first assumption I make, one which seems to stand up to challenge in most dreams, is that everything in a dream is a part of the dreamer. This is a logical assumption to make - our normal sensory apparatus is very much closed to external influences. If we take Jung's position, that dreams arise in the unconscious and have their own language, then it is wise to systematically examine everything that the dream presents us with. This will enable us to by-pass Freud's 'internal censor' and give every dream symbol our full attention. From now on I suggest you play the role of the dream detective, perhaps Sherlock Holmes, and treat no detail as irrelevant.

The first aspect of a dream is what I term 'the Dreamscape'. This is more than just the landscape, since it incorporates elements such as directionology, but, as its name implies, it does form the general backdrop to the dream. It is within the Dreamscape that the actors play their parts and the props are positioned. I divide the Dreamscape into five elements: directionology; the terrain; light and shade; the elements and specific place.

(a) Directionology

I came across directionology as a term used in Feng Shui to refer to the esoteric study of direction. However, the importance of direction and orientation is also found in shamanism (and modern forms such as Wicca) where particular directions are associated with specific qualities, often related to the movement of the sun. Your dream may have explicit references to direction or direction may be inferred (e.g. if you are watching the sunset you are facing west). Here are some of the meanings which have been associated with direction. Please note that the following correspondences do vary with tradition so use your discretion:

East – The sun rises in the east so this direction is related to birth and beginnings. To dream of the east would suggest you are looking at the origins or beginnings of a process. It is also often (though not always) associated with the element of Air which can be linked with thoughts, plans and communication of all kinds. In Feng Shui, the east is symbolised by the azure (or green) dragon.

South – In the northern hemisphere, the sun travels through the southern half of the sky during the day.
In Astrology, the highest part (zenith) of its path is known as the Midheavens and is the area of our life associated with conscious goals. Consequently, to dream of the south focuses us on our

day to day activities and conscious goals. It is often associated with the element of Fire which is linked with enthusiasm, inspiration and strength. If you live in the southern hemisphere, the meanings for south and north should be exchanged. In Feng Shui, the south is symbolised by the red phoenix.

West – The sun sets in the west so this direction is related to death and endings, the conclusion of a process. It is usually associated with the element of Water which can be linked with emotional and artistic issues. In Feng Shui, the west is symbolised by the white tiger.

North – In the northern hemisphere, the sun never enters the northern half of the sky and so dreaming of the north can represent those parts of our life shrouded in shadow. There may be difficult issues to confront in a dream of the north. It is usually associated with the element of Earth which is linked with fertility, money and the manifestation of our hopes and fears. In Feng Shui, the north is symbolised by the black tortoise.

Centre – Dreaming of being at the centre of the four directions suggests the balancing of the strengths and weaknesses associated with the directions.

Directionology deals with orientation on the horizontal plane: In many shamanic traditions, the universe is also split into three vertical levels: the upper, middle and lower worlds. This also fits nicely with psychoanalytic concepts of levels of consciousness and I have found that vertical elevation in dreams provide valuable information on the state of awareness experienced by the dreamer:

Above/Up – Anything above the surface of the earth suggests the known and the conscious. As we move higher we are looking at more refined states of consciousness and spiritual vision.

Below/Down – Anything below the surface of the earth suggests the unknown and the subconscious. Here is where we may encounter aspects of our instinctual nature.

Finally, the relative directions of left and right can be significant.

The Left – Pertains to the part of the mind involved in intuition and psychic and artistic abilities. This part of the mind uses pictures and is able to take a holistic view of things.

The Right – Pertaining to the part of the mind involved in logical thinking, reasoning and intellectual ability. It uses words and is good at discrimination.

An Example:
I dream that I am standing watching the sunset from the top of a cliff. I feel the cliff shaking and start to panic. Looking to my left, I watch a crow performing a strange dance. The cliff crumbles and I fall.

From this hypothetical dream, I would note that I was facing the west (direction of the setting sun) and therefore may be exploring my feelings about death or perhaps something in my life that is coming to an end. I begin the dream from a fully conscious, perhaps even spiritual perspective (on the cliff) but after looking to the left I fall, moving to a more instinctive level. The left symbolises the intuitive, psychic side of life, suggesting that the reasons for this abrupt change in perspective arises from irrational, intuitional promptings (e.g. early negative experiences, spiritual influence) rather than logical thought processes.

I would obviously need to study the crow and its dance for more information but that would be jumping the gun because our dreamscape has not been fully mapped out yet. After making these notes about direction, I would then systematically move on to considering the dream terrain.

(b) The Terrain

Next, I look at the physical landscape within the dream. This can provide me with clues as to the client's experience of life at the time and often represents a general mood that forms the background of the client's life. The type of terrain is inherently neither good nor bad; each provides its own benefits and challenges. Here are some examples:

Flat ground – Life is not challenging at the moment. This can mean you/your client is experiencing either a time of fun and relaxation or instead is dealing with stagnation and boredom.

If interpreting for others it is important to just note down the facts at this stage. Any associated emotions felt by the dreamer will be explored at a later stage. Most importantly, try not to introduce your own prejudice into the interpretation. For example, just because your client is hanging by his fingernails from a skyscraper, don't assume he is feeling fear: he may be an 'adrenaline junkie' for whom such experiences generate euphoria.

Hilly/mountainous ground – Suggests obstacles that the dreamer is facing. If the dreamer is heading towards mountains in the

distance then this is likely to represent a significant challenge which lies ahead.
Forest – Represents the instinctive and feminine sphere of life, a mixture of adventure, security and restriction.

Ocean – Highlights deep, emotional or spiritual issues. The choppier the water, the more disruptive the mood of the dreamer is likely to be.

Of course, the dream may take place completely indoors in which case this part of the analysis can be skipped.

(c) Light and Shade
Next, I look at the lighting of the dream scenario. If the scene is well-lit it indicates that the issues involved are quite open and available to the dreamer's conscious mind.

Conversely, if the dream is dark and murky we are more likely to be dealing with hidden areas of the psyche and the mood of the dreamer may be equally gloomy. Sometimes the dream will move from darkness to light or vice versa and by looking at when this transition occurs we can become aware of what inner or outer events cause our shifts in mood and consciousness.

Famous Dream #4:
Paul McCartney's Yesterday
Yesterday is one of the Beatles' most famous and recognisable hits. It is also remarkable because of the way in which songwriter Sir Paul McCartney discovered it. In 1965, whilst staying in his family home during the filming of Help!, McCartney dreamt he heard a classical ensemble playing a lovely tune. On waking, he sat down at his piano and immediately worked out the tune to Yesterday.

(d) The Elements

The way in which the Greek classical elements (Earth, Air, Fire and Water) appear in dreams supplies further insight into what situations, thoughts, impulses and moods are affecting the dreamer. At this stage, it is a good idea to ask the dreamer what associations they personally make with the relevant elements, since these vary both between and within different traditions.

Also, people may have had significant experiences with the elements that outweigh any traditional correspondences; the element of water is likely to mean something very different to someone who has nearly drowned compared to an Olympic swimmer! Here are some of the more common associations:

Air – The element of air can be present as wind and seems to pertain to our intellectual state and communications with others. A calm, playful breeze can indicate curiosity and sociability while gales and tempests can suggest arguments and a disturbed mind.

Fire – The element of fire may show up in a dream as a blazing hot sun or an erupting volcano, for example. It stands for the instinctive life energy that can either shine forward steadily, bringing strength and warmth to a personality, or become destructive if repressed and then suddenly released (as aggressive anger, for example).

Water – The element of water is common in many dreams and usually represents the state of our emotional lives. Floods and stormy seas indicate the dreamer is dealing with overwhelming feelings while a calm, free flowing river may suggest a poetic, creative phase.

Earth – The element of earth stands for our physical health and connection to the Earth. Some of its significance has already been dealt with in the section on terrain, since the ground we walk on and the contours of the landscape are relevant to this element. We can also look to the features of the surface on which we are walking for further clarification. For example, a sandy surface suggests a lack of emotion in our life while a muddy one indicates too much emotion. A fertile field would suggest the balance is just right.

In the dream example on page ??, the cliff is likely to represent a position of physical security (could be a business, a house or even the dreamer's own body) with the water below giving clues to the dreamer's emotional state. You should ask them about the water: what colour is it? How clean? Is it choppy or calm?
By the way, it doesn't matter if the dreamer doesn't remember the details you are looking for. Just as some witnesses are more reliable than others, some dreamers retain more information than others.

In addition, as I discuss later, one of the fascinating things about working with dreams is that the effort to understand them seems to, of itself, ignite the relationship between dream and dreamer. They will usually find that more (and more vivid) dreams follow in the coming days after an interpretation, along with periods of inspiration and flashbacks. Don't be surprised to receive a call the next day with the dreamer exclaiming, 'The details suddenly came back to me last night. The water was a red, muddy colour... and there were tadpoles in it."

(e) Specific Places and Buildings

Specific places (e.g. villages, towns and cities) represent developed areas of the psyche where we can spend time learning about different aspects of ourselves:

(i) Unfamiliar places:

Sometimes a dreamer might visit a house, village, town or city which has no counterpart in their experience and this suggests they are exploring completely new regions of their psyche.

They may find the situations they face and the activities they are engaged in are far outside those they normally experience.

(ii) Unknown, familiar places:

When new facets of the dreamer's personality are on the verge of coming into consciousness, they may start recognising places which they know they have visited before in their dreams, although they also know they have never actually been there in their everyday lives. As they get more used to the layout of the place, and the people and scenarios which they encounter there, they will be able to remember and explore the symbols more deeply, bringing new skills and knowledge to their waking lives. Particular buildings (e.g. police stations, libraries, hospitals) highlight lessons related to the part of the dreamer that relates to the relevant area (e.g. sense of right and wrong, organisational skills, health, etc.

(iii) Known places:

As the subtitle suggests, these are places which the dreamer knows from their everyday life, even though some details may be different. Here is where they work through common issues, and the identity of the place will be an important indicator about the specific lessons they are working with.

For example, dreaming about a former school or a town in which they once lived might be bringing them back to that period of time to work on issues that arose in that period of their lives. Again, particular buildings (e.g. a workplace, school or social club) relate to specific areas of activity (e.g. work, learning or socialising).

Being in their own home, whether a previous address or a present one, indicates personal matters; the front of the property will represent their public face, that which they reveal to others, while the back will reveal their private identity. The particular room/s they are in are important since it indicates which specific areas of life are being brought up. For example, the kitchen symbolises how we are or were loved and nourished while the bathroom symbolises how we get rid of that which no longer serves us.

CHAPTER 6

MEETING THE ACTOR

This part of the analysis looks specifically at what you, the dreamer in the dream, are doing throughout the dream. It is subdivided into five areas: The actions you perform; your attire (what you're wearing); the words you say; anything out of the ordinary in your behaviour (anomalies) and your feelings and memories.

(a) Actions

Without the social restrictions of everyday life you are more free to act naturally in dreams. The dream source may provoke you by setting up a scenario as a simulation of an everyday situation. For example, if you have issues with anger you may be put in a situation which will trigger your angry reaction, like being criticised by a superior at work. Analysing such dreams can reveal both what is at the root of our anger and the dangerous impulses that could erupt, given free reign.

Always consider that your actions might be metaphorical. For example, if you are throwing a towel in a dream this could indicate that you are giving up on something or someone.

(b) Attire

Clothes are important in dreams because they often represent how you present yourself to others. If you are wearing a formal suit while everyone else is casual then you may feel stiff and awkward in social situations or if you are wearing a protective overall you may feel threatened by the environment. Look ahead at the section on colours as this may be relevant.

Clothes from a particular country or historical period may be referring you to issues regarding a particular place or time. Clothes can reflect a role that you play (e.g. a police uniform) or a specific period in your life (e.g. a school uniform).

(c) Speech

Pay special attention to the words you say within a dream scenario. As explained further in the chapter Tricks & Techniques, the Dream Source uses word play regularly.

If you are puzzled by the words you used in a dream or how you phrased something, check to see if the words or phrases have another meaning that might be relevant.

Famous Dream #5:

Shelley's Vision of Horror

In the summer of 1816, Mary Shelley (then Godwin) and her husband Percy Shelley were invited to Lord Byron's villa on the shores of Lake Geneva. Lord Byron challenged his guests to come up with a ghost story and whilst lying down Mary had

the following vision: 'I saw the pale student of unhallowed arts kneeling beside the thing he had put together. I saw the hideous phantasm of a man stretched out, and then, on the working of some powerful engine, show signs of life...Frightful must it be; for supremely frightful would be the effect of any human endeavour to mock the stupendous Creator...' This chilling image formed the basis of a work which was to become legendary: the story of 'Frankenstein.

(d) Anomalies

One trick that the Dream Source sometimes uses involves compelling us to do or say things we would never normally consider. By looking closely at these anomalies we can sometimes detect the purpose of this interference. For example one lady I spoke to recently sang in public in her dreams. The sense of joy she received from her friends' reactions suggests that she was being shown the benefits of expressing herself to others so that she might experiment with this in 'real' social occasions.

(e) Feelings and Memories

Try to recall what emotions you felt during the dream and directly after waking. Then try and remember when you last felt the same way or in which circumstances similar feelings arise. This can save time in pinpointing what issues your dream is addressing. For example, if you wake up from a recurring dream feeling embarrassed and anxious and you always feel that way in large, social gatherings, then the dreams may be centred on how you handle social situations.

CHAPTER 7

DREAM COMPANIONS

Having covered the general dream background and your own role in the dream we move on to other forms of life that appear in your dream. It may seem odd that I include rocks in this section but I will explain why below.

(a) Rocks and Plants

When interpreting the appearance of rocks and plants, I take a shamanic perspective, one which also fits well with Theosophical views on evolution. Rocks and plants are living 'allies', providing a fixed source of power. To dream of a rock or crystal is usually a message to seek it out in the everyday world.

This is because you might be unable to access the power it contains from within yourself and so you need to bring in the power from an external source. In a sense crystals can be used as 'energy supplements'. Dreaming of a plant can either be a message to obtain the physical plant for healing purposes or can be more symbolic (e.g. dreaming of ivy can symbolise being overly attached to someone).

To determine the uses and symbolic meanings of crystals/rocks and plants I would advise looking in a good book on crystals, shamanism or druidry.

(b) Animals

Animals often feature in dreams, especially those of children. There are clearly countless animals which could appear in a dream but once their generic meaning is established they become easier to interpret. Animals in dreams seem to represent our instinctive nature, those parts of the psyche we have not fully integrated. When dreaming of animals, ask yourself what is this creature renowned for, either in the natural world or in folklore. For example, frogs are associated with transformation since, not only do they change appearance significantly during development, but they also often change into princes in our fairy tales. The more obscure the animal, the more important it is to find out exactly what its special talents or mythical associations are. When you have come up with some ideas try to relate those attributes to yourself and study the dream for clues as to how these fit in with the rest of the dream. As with rocks and plants, shamans regard animals they encounter in 'non-ordinary reality' as potential 'allies' or 'power animals'.

Famous Dream #6:
Kekule's Snake

Kekule (full name Friedrich August Kekule von Stradonitz) said to his colleagues, "Let us learn to dream!" He became a fan of dreaming after coming up with his Structural Theory of organic chemistry with the help of vivid daydreams involving dancing atoms. He also solved the confounding problem of the structure of benzene. He was, as usual, daydreaming, visualising chains of molecules dancing in a snake-like manner. Suddenly: "One of the snakes had seized hold of its own tail." Not only did he work out from this that Benzene forms a ring but he had also encountered a classic dream symbol, the oroubouros.

(c) People

Although there are occasions when other people do seem to enter our dreams, most of the time when we encounter other people, we are meeting our own sub-personalities: dream people are not normally real people. This should not surprise us since even in our 'objective' waking life we co-create other people by constantly and automatically projecting parts of our own psyche onto them. Logically, the dream image of a real-life person is even more coloured by our own psyches. Jung described a dream person as a, "complex of psychic factors that has fashioned itself."(p53).

Some dream characters are encountered by people across time and different cultures and Jung believed them to be fundamental principles that resided in the collective unconscious. According to Jung, these dream characters have a plastic form and maintain their own autonomous existence which extends beyond individual psyches; he called them the 'mythologems' or 'archetypes'. To my mind, the archetypes are powerful, transpersonal forces that rise up from the collective unconscious. In trying to grapple with these forces, our psyche cloaks them in symbols which evoke certain facets of their nature. However, since the forces in their entirety are beyond our ability to conceptualise we are left with a feeling of great power and mystery.

(i) The Archetypes

There are lots of different archetypal characters, some of which I'll mention below, but the three major archetypes are, as follows:

The Shadow:

This character is really a partial archetype since it is partially created by the individual. During early childhood we are extremely dependant on our caregivers and from an early age we learn which behaviours are acceptable and which are not. Those aspects of ourselves, denied their natural expression, are stored away in our unconscious mind and are added to, as we develop, by other things that are repressed or merely forgotten.

According to Jung, these hidden qualities form the personal part of the 'shadow' archetype, an alter-ego which haunts our dreams and occasionally erupts into daily life when our guard is down. The shadow is elusive and can appear in our dreams as a vague, threatening presence, a frightening villain or just someone we intensely dislike. Facing the shadow is one of the most healing things we can do and as we integrate its qualities it becomes less 'dense'. The less we know about our shadow, the more free access it has to project its perceived faults onto others, damaging our relationships.

The Anima and Animus:

The complete anima has been described as 'every experience a man has ever had with any woman' and she appears in a man's dream as an influential woman. Likewise, the animus is 'every experience a woman has ever had with any man', appearing in a woman's dream as an influential man. Jung saw integrating these archetypes as more tricky than dealing with the shadow since they have never been part of us but are the source of our attraction to the opposite sex. In our dreams this archetype can appear in many guises, some positive, some negative. By learning from these characters we can learn to give voice to qualities usually associated with the other sex.

(ii) Unknown people

Unknown characters usually represent sub-personalities of which we are unaware. Each stranger is potentially a source of information on how we can bring new abilities into our waking lives or, if the characters are unpleasant, how we can learn to understand our negative traits and reduce the risk of displaying them. Some unknown characters are archetypal and, if Jung was correct, represent universal principles. Such archetypes include the Earth mother, the wise man, the higher self, the hero, the villain, the tramp and the sorcerer. They may bring powerful philosophical and spiritual messages.

(iii) Known people

During a dream, family members are usually your representation of their qualities and vices, internalised during our childhood. In a traditional family, the father may represent our voice of reason and conscience while the mother might be our source of love and nourishment. When dreaming of family members try and decide what role they play or have played in the formation of your personality. If there is conflict in the dream then there may be an internal dilemma over which approach to take.

When meeting friends and acquaintances in dreams, think of a word or two that you would use to describe them. They are likely to be symbolic of the part of your personality that is like them.

CHAPTER 8

A MULTITUDE OF OBJECTS

Of course, the variety of inanimate objects which could and do appear in dreams are limitless, especially considering the novel combinations made by mixing objects together. Although I look at inanimate objects last, it is often with their consideration that some of the most important dream information comes to light.

For example, in one of my own dreams I had failed a driving test, quite a common theme in dreams. I had looked at the location of the dream and the people involved which had enlightened me as to which of life's lessons I was currently failing but one final, easily overlooked detail provided a crucial piece of information. The examiner had marked his sheet in pencil. Had I not been using the LIF I would have almost certainly glossed over this detail.

However, during the 'Objects' phase of interpretation, I realised that this detail was telling me that my mistakes would not have a lasting effect - they could be erased.

One special class of object which seems to feature a lot in dreams - mine, at least - are vehicles. Cars seem to be naturally symbolic of motivation and drive with walking and cycling symbolising self-motivated action which requires exertion. Passenger vehicles such as trains, planes and buses often relate to career while lorries highlight a burden being carried.

(a) Colour

I have put colours inside a separate sub-section because of their vital importance in dream interpretation. The meanings of colours, while being highly individual, do seem to contain a large degree of shared meaning, as follows:

Red – Anger, passion
Yellow – Intellect, positivity, communication
Orange – Sensuality, joy
Green – Health, growth (envy if murky)
Indigo – Clairvoyance
Violet – Spirituality, religion, spiritual healing
Light blue – Freedom, clairaudience, vocal expression
Black – Protection, fear
White – Protection, spirituality
Brown – The mundane, fertility
Grey – Illusion, confusion, deception

Famous Dream #7:

Madame Walker's Special Formula

Madame C.J. Walker became the first self-made female millionaire in the USA. Her secret? She dreamt the ingredients for a hair restoration formula. I'm guessing alopecia was widespread at the time.

CHAPTER 9

ASTROLOGY & MYTHOLOGY: DREAMS FROM THE COLLECTIVE UNCONSCIOUS

If Jung is fundamentally correct, then some of our most profound dreams have their source in the Collective Unconscious. Although Jung's early definition of the Collective Unconscious was more biological than mystical, the term has come to be associated with esoteric notions of a shared group mind, an idea that may well have been accepted by Jung during his later, more spiritual years.

Either way, Jung believed that the archetypes not only appeared in the dreams of all humanity but, unsurprisingly, became enshrined in our art and mythology as motifs or 'mythologems' (Jung, p.79).

In fact, Jung went as far as to state that a knowledge of folklore and mythology is essential if we are to attempt to grasp the meaning of those powerful and mysterious dreams which formed part of a client's process of individuation (Jung, p. 78).

Famous Dream #8:

Dream Teaches Howe to Sew

In 1945, inventor Elias Howe was designing a sewing machine but he was unsure exactly where to put the hole in the needle. His problem was solved one night after he dreamt of being attacked by warriors with odd-looking weapons: spears with holes just above their tips.

Astrology

Given the above, it is not surprising to find that astrology, a belief system which has surfaced in many different cultures throughout time, can feature in our dreams. Those with experience in astrology may be especially sensitive to the appearance of astrological symbols, but as an aid to recognising their appearance in dreams, I present below a list of the astrological signs, together with their ruling planets and common correspondences. For a more comprehensive list of symbols it would be advisable to dip into one or two good astrological books.

If you believe the dream is astrological in nature, most good astrological books (or a search online) will provide an overview of the characteristics of the sign you are interested in.

Aries – Ruled by Mars (The ram, colour red, iron)
Taurus – Ruled by Venus (The bull, pink and pale blue, copper)
Gemini – Ruled by Mercury (The twins, yellow, mercury metal)
Cancer – Ruled by the Moon (The crab, the dog, silver, pearl, the fresh spring)

Leo – Ruled by the Sun (The lion, gold)
Virgo – Ruled by Mercury (The virgin, natural greens and browns)
Libra – Ruled by Venus (The scales, law, relationships, pink, green)
Scorpio – Ruled by Pluto or Mars (The scorpion, black, plutonium, iron, volcanoes, the still pool)
Sagittarius – Ruled by Jupiter (The centaur, sky blue, philosophy, the arrow, tin)
Capricorn – Ruled by Saturn (The goat, natural browns, greens, greys and black, lead, the scythe)
Aquarius – Ruled by Uranus and Saturn (The water carrier, social causes, detachment, science, electricity, aqua blue, uranium)
Pisces – Ruled by Neptune (The two fish, sea green and blue, the trident, the ocean)

Religion & Mythology

During your dream work, you might come across characters and themes from a wide range of cultural mythologies, religions and art forms. These are archetypal themes which surface from the collective unconscious. For example the quest for the Holy Grail, the battle between good and evil, flood myths and the temptation of the hero are all archetypal themes which surface again and again in various guises in dreams.

One interesting thing I have found as a tarot reader is that I have occasionally come across dreams which embody the same symbols as the tarot cards, especially those of the major arcana. In fact, in one case I interpreted a dream which included every single one of the symbols associated with a particular major tarot card despite the fact that the client had no prior experience with the tarot.

This dream suggested to me that some, if not all, dreams are holistic in nature and that every symbol, whether recognised or not, ties in with the message that is being communicated.

Again, if you believe the dream you are working on is related to a cultural story or a religious text, then it would be wise to find a trustworthy source on the relevant tradition to inform your interpretation. In general, the more informed you become in these areas the more effective your interpretations are likely to be.

CHAPTER 10

CLASSIC DREAM THEMES

There are some dreams which it seems everyone has experienced at one time or another. They are related to archetypal themes and I have picked three of them for this section.

(a) Teeth falling out

One of my pet hates in dream interpretation is the use of the blanket phrase 'anxiety dream' or 'insecurity dream' in order to explain away a wide variety of dreams, each unique to every individual and each containing subtle differences which can greatly aid interpretation.

Yes, dreaming of teeth falling out is clearly an anxiety dream (unless you do not feel anxious when dreaming it). However, the particular symbol of teeth relates equally clearly to growth and change. Looking back through my old journals, I came across a dream where my two incisors had fallen out. Soon after, my partner's pregnancy test showed she was pregnant with our first child - that was certainly a big change!

The teeth are one of the only parts of the body that provide a physical marker of growth and age. Our teeth fall out during childhood to mark our movement away from suckling and into independence and also during old age, a reminder of the reality of death. Dreaming of teeth falling out seems to happen when we are anxious specifically about a transition in our lives; it is related to the Tarot card of Death and the Astrological sign of Capricorn.

Famous Dream #9:

Niklaus's New Swing

In 1964, golfing star Jack Niklaus dreamt of an alternative grip to use in his golf swing. After adopting the dream technique, his scores improved dramatically.

(b) Being naked in public

Going back to the section on attire, being naked (again usually an anxiety dream) highlights that we are very open and naive when expressing ourselves. If the dreamer does feel anxious in this type of dream I would advise being more guarded when in social situations.

Coincidentally, shortly before typesetting this page, I had a dream where I was naked from the waist down in public.

(c) Being chased (sometimes unable to move)

When we are being chased in a dream, it is very likely that we are fleeing the Shadow archetype. This is the part of us which we refuse to accept because it contains all of our unwanted vices.

In Jung's theory, the Shadow becomes an autonomous part of the psyche - basically, a real entity in itself.

Facing the Shadow is one of the most healing things we can do in our dreams because we have the opportunity to regain lost talents that we may have bundled up with our deep-rooted fears. For example, an angry and violent murderer in our dreams may also contain positive aspects such as assertiveness and self-preservation.

Facing the Shadow is related to the theme of the Strength card in the Tarot and surfaces in numerous myths and art forms wherever a confrontation between the hero and arch-villain occurs. The inability to move may be a dim awareness of the physical paralysis that accompanies most people's dreaming state.

An explanation of sleep paralysis and its association with OOBEs can be found in the writings of Robert Bruce and his concept of what actually happens during an out of body experience are definitely worth considering.

CHAPTER 11

FROM NUMBERS TO NIGHTMARES

Word Play

In my experience, the Dream Source has a particular penchant for word play. Even as far back as Ancient Egyptian times, interpreters realised that certain symbols were related to certain themes purely because of similarities in the words. For example, the words for 'donkey' and 'great' were homonyms in that language (had the same spelling and sound), so to dream of a donkey was a sign of good fortune. Pay special attention to any use of language in a dream, whether written or spoken, even if you are the one saying or writing it. Ask yourself if the word or phrase has an alternative meaning.

Here are some examples from my own dreams:

I once had a dream where I told a man that I was studying for my BSc (a British university qualification). The man replied that he had only achieved his "c". On the surface, this seemed a bizarre and irrelevant comment until I later realised the character was referring to the word "see" which corresponded with many other symbols involving eyes and seeing, and led me to a satisfactory interpretation.

Another dream revolved around themes of subservience and people-pleasing. It was a disturbing dream from several years back that I was revisiting. A character in the scene was someone I vaguely knew called Mrs. Bowden. I suddenly realised that the reason she was in my dream was purely semantic due to the similarity to the phrase 'bow down'. This example also highlights the value of returning to old dreams with a fresh pair of eyes.

Another favourite dream of mine - and one for the sceptics - was a very short scene depicting a puzzled looking man peering at the bumper of his VW Beetle following a minor collision.

I woke up (in the real world), and wondered what this brief dream could possibly mean. I walked downstairs and turned on the TV. The news was on and the very first sentence out of the newscaster's mouth was, "It's difficult to see the impact this will have on Volkswagen".

Number Games

Numbers, spoken or written, often make an appearance in dreams. You may immediately pick up on their significance (if they relate to an important date, for example) or they may seem completely random.

If it is the latter case, one method of exploring their meaning is to 'free associate' with your client (or yourself). Jung devoted chapter two of *Dreams* to numbers and worked through several examples of the method he used to arrive at the latent meaning attached to them.

The technique is to break down any complex numbers into their constituent parts and relate these numbers to life events, no matter how tenuous the links may seem.

For example, one of my dreams presented me with the numbers 759216. Maybe I should have done the lottery that night, but instead I free associated with the numbers and came up with the following:

7 – Days in a week
5 – Wore the Number 5 shirt in football today
9 – 999 emergency
2 – Twice replaced as a linesman
1 – Only one mistake
6 – Days until my next match

Added = 30 – Degrees in an astrological sign

I had played and officiated at a football match that afternoon, and it was clearly still very much on my mind. This would be a good place to start the interpretation.

Nagging (The Recurring Dream)
If the Dream Source wants to work with you on a particular issue, it may attract your attention with a recurring dream (I call it a 'nagging dream'). This may be exactly the same dream each time or there may be slight differences.

When you start taking the dream seriously, subsequent dreams are likely to have very subtle differences which give a clear indication of the process you are working through and what approaches you should adopt or avoid. The issues involved are often complex and the Dream Source will take you step by step through their resolution.

Famous Dream #10:

Namakkal's Nightly Lessons

Most people would prefer to avoid homework, even when it comes in a dream courtesy of a goddess. For mathematical genius Srinivasa Ramanujan, however, goddess Namakkal's regular visits helped him to prove over 3,000 theorems in his lifetime. She even livened things up by presenting some equations in blood!

Red Alert! (The Nightmare)

If an issue is particularly important, and you show no sign of listening to subtle messages from your unconscious, the Dream Source will often shake you up with a nightmare. This performs two functions. First, you are likely pay attention to it, and second, you will probably ask others around you what it might mean, opening up the message to those around you. Jung described nightmares as having, "a dramatic structure which aims logically at creating a highly affective situation" (p.40).

Frightening characters in your dreams are often a backlash from the repressed parts of your personality, the 'shadow archetype' discussed earlier.

CHAPTER 12

INTERPRETING FOR OTHERS: THE GUIDELINES

"Everyone who analyses the dreams of others should constantly bear in mind that there is no simple and generally known theory of psychic phenomena"
-Carl Gustav Jung-

If you decide to take the framework and apply it to others, there are a few things that you need to bear in mind.

One of the most important factors to be aware of is the psychological phenomenon of projection. We are naturally accustomed to dealing with other people as if we know a great deal about them, and our ability to utilise a 'theory of mind' usually serves us well in judging the basic emotional states and motivations of others. But when we move from everyday interactions to psychological investigations, we seem to be conditioned to unconsciously see parts of our own psyche in other people, particularly if those parts are distasteful to us. For example, if we have anger issues bubbling beneath the surface we are likely to see other people as hostile to us.

Talented dream interpreter Jonathan Zap explains: "Projection can be the grossest and most obvious of psychological phenomena but also the subtlest, most elusive, slipperiest and inscrutable. To some extent, all perception is to 'look through a glass darkly' and often to see a distorted reflection of your own psychic structure when you think you are objectively seeing something external". (If you are reading the eBook, you can click this link to read the full Jonathan Zap article).

In relation to dream interpretation, one warning sign that we are projecting is a tendency to feel frustration if your client doesn't immediately comprehend the insights you have revealed. If you intend your interpretation to be of benefit to your client, your main task is to help them to understand their own dream, not to impose your own theories, no matter how reasonable, on them. Your clients' psychological realities will be very different from your own and dream symbols will have a unique personal resonance with each dreamer. The antidote to projection is to be as objective as possible in your interpretation: stick to the facts of the dream and work with your clients' associations, using your own only to provide possible new material. If the dreamer is struggling to understand their symbols, don't force anything: it is not unusual for a client to reach a breakthrough through further dreams and/or waking experiences. In fact, individual dreams often form part of a series.

Jung would analyse hundreds of dreams from the same client and found that they revealed an ongoing process of individuation (see Jung p.77). He theorised that the whole of human evolution may be about the development of a self which could successfully integrate both the conscious and unconscious aspects of the psyche.

Note that if your suggestions are at odds with your client's cherished image of him or herself, they might be offended. Jung notes, 'the dreamer, like most people, usually displays an astonishing sensitiveness to critical remarks… even more if they are right' (Jung p.71). He goes on to explain, 'the dream describes the inner situation of the dreamer, but the conscious mind denies its truth and reality or admits it only grudgingly.' (Jung p.90).

So how should you question your client? First of all, Jung suggests reminding yourself that you have no idea what the dream means, ensuring that you begin the process in as detached and objective a manner as possible.

You should always make full use of the contextual material provided by the dreamer; in other words, find out as much as you can about their current life, what problems or successes they are having, the state of their relationships, etc. Some people will be more open to divulging sensitive information than others. This, of course, is fine but can make your task harder. The best technique to use seems to be similar to the psychoanalytic technique of 'free association'.

Following the structure of the framework, continually ask the dreamer what he or she associates with the symbols that arise. Ask them to say the first things that come to mind, no matter how irrelevant they seem; sometimes, the least obvious clues are the ones that lead to a breakthrough. They may come out with single words, phrases or entire anecdotes. For example, dreaming of eggs may suggest 'birth' or 'nature' or 'don't put all your eggs in one basket'. Or it may bring your client back to a time when they helped Uncle Giles out at the farm.

The Felt Sense

I believe that Gendlin's 'felt sense' is the same as Jung's 'surge of affect' (Jung p.56)

Finally, I would caution anyone against attempting to analyse dreams that are clearly 'flashbacks' to previous traumatic experiences. Jung believed that such dreams were split-off parts of the personality and would continue to reproduce themselves until the traumatic material could be reintegrated. He found no value in interpreting them and I would be inclined to trust his experience.

CHAPTER 13

BEYOND DREAMING

Pushing the Boundaries

Up to now, I have stuck to the hypothesis that dreams arise in a hidden part of our psyche - the unconscious - and have their own symbolic language. As a tool, the interpretation framework I have created has served me well, enabling me to shed light on a variety of dreams from the most straightforward and banal to the highly complex and profound. Hopefully it will enable you to do the same.

But not every dream experience seems to fit neatly into the hypothesis above, and there are phenomena associated with dreaming that throw up interesting and sometimes unsettling questions. This section attempts to provide an overview of some of these phenomena. For example, what is lucid dreaming and does it actually happen? What happens to us during an out of body experience?

What is the difference between dreaming, shamanic journeying and pathworking? Can dreams and 'real life' influence each other? What is synchronicity? Do dreams predict the future? In short, what happens when 'dreams' meet 'reality'?

Lucid Dreams

For most people, at least most of the time, dreams are a fairly passive phenomenon. Although we play a role in the dream, we are completely caught up in its reality, only becoming aware of the fact we were dreaming after we wake. Lucid (or conscious) dreams are those dreams in which we maintain (or recover) some conscious awareness of the fact that we are dreaming. In short, we 'wake up' within our dreams. Lucid dreams seem to be on a continuum ranging from a dim sense of objective awareness to the ability to achieve complete control over our actions and even the contents of our dream experience. This may seem a bizarre notion to those who have never experienced a lucid dream but they do happen and, furthermore, since the 1980s they have been rigorously studied. The person most famous for studying lucid dreams is psychophysiologist Stephen LaBerge, founder of the Lucidity Institute and pioneer of a clever technique (though not the first of such techniques) whereby lucid dreamers can use special eye movement signals from within their dreams in order to communicate with experimenters.

Famous Dream #11:

Robert Louis Stevenson

If lucid dreaming were an art form, then Stevenson would have been a grand master. He used dreaming as a major part of his creative process and could dream scenes and entire plots, even returning to previous dreams in order to change their endings. His extraordinary dream life helped him to turn his idea for 'Dr Jeckyll and Mr Hyde' into a published book in just ten weeks.

OOBEs

I mentioned Out of Body Experiences (OOBEs) earlier in the book and due to my personal experiences with them I can say with certainty that the state of consciousness is indistinguishable from the waking state. So are OOBEs really evidence that a part of us can actually leave the body? Or are they just a special kind of lucid dream?

There have been studies on Near Death Experiences (NDEs), a type of OOBE that occurs naturally when the body faces death, and some of the evidence is compelling. For example, health professionals in operating theatres have sometimes vouched for the accuracy of details relayed by NDE experiencers about what was happening around them during their operations. Part of the work of the Monroe Institute in Virginia, USA, is in trying to address this question objectively.

Paul Devereux, in his fascinating book *Shamanism and the Mystery Lines*, brings up the issue with a number of OOBE researchers. Having experienced OOBEs himself, Devereux finds it difficult to believe that nothing leaves the body but he does concede that the difference between a particularly convincing lucid dream and a full-blown OOBE is hard to explain.

One possible alternative explanation is articulated by psychologist Susan Blackmore. She argues that an OOBE is the brain's way of trying to maintain a body-centred perspective in the absence of sensation or when to be 'in the body' is traumatic (e.g., during death, accident or abuse). In her view, an OOBE is a 'metachoric' experience: an example of the mind's ability to create convincing hallucinatory experiences.

The Shamanic Journey

I have already mentioned a little about the shamanic perspective on dreaming but how does a shamanic 'journey' compare with a daydream, a structured meditation (e.g., pathworking), a lucid dream and an OOBE. This is a difficult question since people vary in both their approach to and their experience of journeying. However, in general, a journey begins in the waking state (like a daydream) and follows a structured pattern (like a self-guided meditation). One of the key elements to a journey is the use of techniques, such as drumming, to induce a particular state of consciousness. At a certain stage in the journey, the shift will be made from one level of awareness (the ordinary) to another, where experiences are more dream-like (the non-ordinary). Therefore, shamanic journeying and lucid dreaming may only differ in form and focus with the former being practised within a particular belief system with the aim of contacting spiritual forces for healing and knowledge. In addition, for a journey to be 'shamanic' there is an implicit understanding that something is leaving the physical body so that all such experiences are by definition believed to be OOBEs.

Synchronicity

Throughout this book, I have mentioned C.G. Jung's theories of the collective unconscious and the archetypes. Another theory he is famous for is the acausal connecting principle, a principle he termed synchronicity. Through his experiences and studies, Jung came to believe that alongside the accepted connecting process of cause and effect, there worked another process which connected similar events. In the book he presents his famous case study whereby a young female client, at a critical moment of her treatment, was recounting a dream of a golden scarab. Jung heard a tapping at the window and saw a flying insect at the window. On opening the window, the insect flew in and he caught it. It was a scarabaeid beetle which, according to Jung, was the nearest analogy to a golden scarab to be found in the local area. Jung goes on to elaborate on both the significance of the symbolism and its timing.

Many people have anecdotes about significant coincidences in their lives and often such anecdotes involve dreams. If we are to consider that dreams can sometimes spill out into our lives then it may be worth asking another question: can dreams predict the future?

Premonition

One Saturday night I dreamt I was walking up a lane with my son. We came to a gap in the hedge over which I could see a horse. "Oh, look! A horse." I said, to which my son laughed and replied, 'That's not a horse, it's a camel.' I looked again and, sure enough, he was right.

The next day, we were visiting my son's grandfather's house. My son picked up a merry-go-round toy and brought it over to show me. 'Look!' he said. I glanced at the toy and the brightly painted horses. 'Oh yes, horses.' I said, to which my son laughed and said, 'They're not horses. They're camels.' He was right.

To a scientist, this would be an example of an anecdote: a single 'case study' performed by a lay person. It can't be repeated and it can't be controlled, hence it could never be provided as evidence that dreams can foretell events in waking life. To me, however, this is strong evidence. This is not my only experience of predictive dreams: I have met two people in my dreams before meeting them in real life, and I have had numerous dreams which, on hindsight, had much in common with significant world events. One of the frustrating things about predictive dreams are that they are very rare, often heavily symbolised and don't seem to be at all correlated with the significance of external events. Jung saw in such dreams evidence of a prospective function. He believed that they came about due to a synthesis of conscious and subliminal material, including consciously forgotten memories (cryptamnesia).

One special case of prospective dream is the premonition of death. One notable example is Abraham Lincoln' alleged premonition (see box below). Personally, I believe premonitions do occur but the elusive rules by which they operate and the difficulty of testing them means they remain one of the Dream Source's great mysteries.

Famous Dream #12:
Lincoln's Premonition
President Abraham Lincoln (1809-1865) attached great importance to his dreams. One night, he dreamt that he was in bed at the White House and heard people sobbing. He went from room to room, unable to locate the source of the sound. Eventually, he entered the East Room where he saw a body laid out, surrounded by soldiers. "Who is dead in the White House?" he asked. "The President," a soldier replied. "He was killed by an assassin." Days after recounting this dream to his bodyguard, actor and confederate spy John Wilkes Booth shot Lincoln dead.

Moving Forward: Interpreting Life
I initially started interpreting my own and others' dreams out of curiosity, but one of the lessons I learned early on is that the Dream Source doesn't seem to be content to stand still for long. I had just got to grips with incubating and working on my own

dreams when, almost immediately, I began to get dreams which didn't make sense until I bumped into somebody else - often a work colleague. Frequently, the message of the dream was not meant for me at all but made perfect sense to someone else. I began to feel that I was being called upon to help in the lives of others, to take part in a project that transcended my own personal interests and concerns.

My journey, which had begun with an out of body experience, had led me to places where people travel to other realities and speak to spirits, where dreams speak of the future and of other people's lives, and where golden beetles travel from the unconscious mind to land on psychiatrists' windows. I had moved from simply interpreting dreams to using dreams as another tool in attempting the vast challenge that has faced mankind since the day we became conscious of our own existence: the challenge of interpreting life. I now stood on the brink of a new world view, a view where the everyday distinction between inner and outer, real and dream was breaking down. Only I soon realised that this world view was not 'new' at all. In fact, it was a return to the primal world view that we all shared before the Enlightenment.

CHAPTER 14

AFTERWORD

Returning to the primal world view

Richard Tarnas, in his brilliant book *Cosmos and Psyche*, talks of how the evolution of the modern world view has been characterised by the steady objectification of the external world. In an attempt to know the world empirically, we have gradually withdrawn all intrinsic meaning from that world and appropriated it for ourselves, becoming convinced that only we are capable of attributing significance and meaning - surely the ultimate arrogance.

Consequently, we now find ourselves alone and adrift in a soulless universe. When our dreams speak to us, we regard them as purposeless mental chatter, and if we dare suggest that the world outside is speaking to us through omens and strange coincidences, we are treated as naive or eccentric, perhaps even ill.

But if we are prepared to dig beneath the surface, to look at our ancient history and to listen to those who still live by its wisdom, we can rediscover an age old way of understanding. We can open our eyes to a primal world view that sees no separation between inner and outer, that experiences a universe which communicates with us constantly because it too is conscious and because it is part of us and we are part of it. In this world everything is related to everything else so that we can look out at the stars and planets, inwards to our dreams or down at a spread of cards or a scatter of yarrow stalks, and know ourselves because we are all part of one great whole.

Tarnas says that 'world views create worlds'. If this is true, then we need to choose carefully which world view we want to live by. Will we follow the view that the world is devoid of importance, there to be used for our own ends? Or will we instead choose to believe that the universe and ourselves are one, indivisible whole.

I believe the whole human story is epitomised by the great archetypal quest: a journey where we strike out to achieve independence and to realise our destinies. In many such stories, the hero or heroine eventually realises that their ultimate destiny is to return home a wiser soul.

Perhaps it's time for us all to embrace the primal world view, to listen to the Universe, to gather up our belongings and return home.

BE YOUR OWN DREAM DETECTIVE

References/Further Reading

Conscious Dreaming by Robert Moss, Crown Trade Paperbacks (1996)

10,000 Dreams Interpreted/Quantum Dream Dictionary by Pamela Ball, Herron Books/Quantum (2003)

Let Your Body Interpret Your Dreams by Eugene Gendlin, Chiron Publications (1986)

The Interpretation of Dreams by Sigmund Freud, MacMillan Co. (1937)

Dreams by C.G. Jung, Princeton University Press (1974)

The Archetypes and the Collective Unconscious by C.G. Jung, Princeton University Press (1934-1954)

Synchronicity: An Acausal Connecting Principle by C.G. Jung, Princeton University Press (1973)

Shamanism and the Mystery Lines by Paul Devereux, Quantum (2001)

Cosmos and Psyche by Richard Tarnas, Plume (2007)

GLOSSARY OF TERMS

10,000 Dreams Interpreted/Quantum Dream Dictionary (book): Written by Pamela Ball, *10,000 Dreams Interpreted* provides a concise introduction to Jungian Psychology including the Collective Unconscious and the Archetypes. It offers various levels of interpretation for a comprehensive list of dream symbols and is a good reference work to use alongside the LIF®.

Analytical Psychology: Used interchangeably with the term Jungian psychology. It revolves around the individual psyche and its drive towards integration of its many fragmented parts.

Anima: One of the most important Jungian archetypes. It is traditionally explained as the feminine principle within the unconscious psyche of the male. However, this may be rejected by readers who view gender as non-binary. As part of the collective unconscious, the anima is transpersonal but, according to Jung, takes on characteristics based on the male's experience with females (usually beginning with the mother). Integration with the anima is important to avoid relationships becoming based on its projection on to other women. In dreams, the anima comes in many guises but is perceived as one female entity.

Animus: One of the most important Jungian archetypes. It is traditionally explained as the masculine principle within the unconscious psyche of the female. However, this may be rejected by readers who view gender as non-binary. As part of the collective unconscious, the anima is transpersonal but, according to Jung, takes on characteristics based on the female's experience with males (usually beginning with the father). Integration with the anima is important to avoid relationships becoming based on its projection on to other men. In dreams, the anima comes in many guises and is perceived as several different male entities.

Archetypes: The archetypes of Carl Gustav Jung are primordial instincts which reside in and arise from the collective unconscious. They are transpersonal but give rise to archetypal images within the human psyche. It is these, according to Jung, that influence our personal psychologies and are projected as myths and art forms. Among the most powerful of the archetypes are the shadow, anima and animus and the main work of analytical psychology is integrating these archetypes with our conscious awareness as much as is possible.

Asclepeions: In Ancient Greece, asclepeions were temple dedicated to Asclepius, the God of Medicine. People would visit the temples for physical and spiritual healing. They would sometimes sleep in the temples and receive guidance through their dreams - one of the earliest examples of dream incubation.

Asclepius: Greek god of healing. His symbol, the snake-entwined rod, is still prominent in the medical profession. One of his daughters, Panacea, gave us the word for a substance which cures all ills.

Aserinsky, Eugine: The son of a Russian-Jewish dentist, Aserinsky was one of the pioneers of modern dream research. Together with his supervisor Nathaniel Kleitman, Aserinsky first linked REM sleep with dreaming following experiments carried out in the dream laboratories of Chicago.

Astrology: The ancient belief system that relates personal and world events and characteristics to the relative positions of the planets, constellations and other heavenly bodies (the sun, the moon, asteroids, etc.) In Western astrology, the 'heavens' are divided into 12 'signs', each named after 12 nearby constellations. In turn, each of the signs are ruled by one or more planets/

heavenly bodies. Astrological symbols such as the signs, planets and associated qualities may appear in dreams.

Ball, Pamela: Author of *10,000 Dreams Interpreted/The Quantum Dream Dictionary*. Born in Hawaii, Ball has worked in America and Europe writing on dreams, natural magic and psychic research.

Bruce, Robert: Australian author Bruce is an expert in Out of Body Experiences (OOBEs) and has created numerous works based on his experiential approach to studying them.

Celestite: A crystal used in dream incubation for improving dream recall. It consists of strontium sulfate and is a delicate blue colour.

Censor: Described by Sigmund Freud as a force dedicated to keeping unwanted tendencies out of conscious awareness. When psychotherapists attempt to bring these tendencies into the open during therapy, they will encounter resistance from the patient as the censor acts to keep the unwanted tendencies in the unconscious. In dreams, the censor is weakened but still active. Instead of blocking the unwanted tendencies, it softens or alters them.

Collective unconscious: A theory developed by Carl Gustav Jung. It suggests that humanity as a whole is influenced by transpersonal forces in the form of instincts and developed structures he termed archetypes. Archetypes and the Collective Unconscious itself impinge upon consciousness in the form of powerful dream symbols.

Condensation: One of the ways in which the censor blocks repressed material from conscious awareness, during dreams, is by combining two or more unwanted tendencies into one dream symbol. This psychoanalytic process is termed condensation.

Deir-el-Medina: The Ancient Egyptian village in which scribe Kenhirkhopeshef's book of dreams was discovered. The scribe used the book over 1000 years BC, and the book is thought to have been ancient even then. It is one of the first examples of oneirology - the attempt to interpret dreams. This ability was credited to Joseph, an important Biblical figure who rose from captivity to become vizier of Egypt.

Derment, William C.: Working under his supervisor Nathaniel Kleitman, William C. Dement was one of the three people credited with pioneering the discipline of scientific sleep research. Fellow University of Chicago undergraduate Eugene Aserinsky, together with Kleitman, first identified REM sleep with Aserinsky suggesting that this phase may be associated with dreaming. Dement and Kleitman moved the research forward and proved the link between dreams and REM sleep.

Directionology: Directionology is a belief system shared between various traditions (including native American shamanism, European witchcraft and feng shui). It assigns various symbols and characteristics to spatial directions (e.g., north, east, south, west, above and below). An example of directionology is the association of the west with death and endings based upon the phenomenon of the setting sun in that direction. Directionology is used in the LIF® for interpreting dreams.

Displacement: One of the ways in which the censors blocks repressed material from conscious awareness during dreams. It projects the unwanted tendencies on to a misleading dream symbol, taking conscious attention away from its true meaning. Freud uses the example of his dream, 'Irma's Injection', to illustrate the displacement of his latent anger towards a negligent colleague (Fleiss) on to a completely different colleague (Otto) who becomes the misleading manifest dream symbol.

Dream incubation: The process of alerting the Dream Source (or the subconscious mind, depending on one's belief system) of the intent to interpret dreams. Dream incubation may involve rituals and tools such as crystals or can consist merely of telling yourself to remember your dreams and recording these in a bedside dream journal. Dream incubation appears to increase the frequency of dreams and the strength of dream recall. It is recommended for people using the LIF® to interpret their own dreams.

Dream journal: A book used solely for the recording and interpretation of dreams. Keeping a dream journal in itself seems to act as a catalyst for rich dream experiences and can be therefore thought of as a basic form of dream incubation.

Dream Source: I chose the Dream Source as a neutral term to cover most belief systems while causing the least upset or controoversy. For scientific rationalists, the Dream Source might be thought of as the meaningless effects of brain processes. For psychoanalysts, the Dream Source would be the interplay between forces and tendencies within the psyche. If you are religious, you might think of the Dream Source as God, the Goddess or Thoth, depending on your beliefs. In New Age and Jungian thought, the Dream Source might translate as the Higher Self - a spiritual or archetypal force. I personally experience the Dream Source as a highly intelligent and aware autonomous force that uses dreams to help me understand myself and life itself.

Dream Symbols: Anything, including people and elements of the landscape, that appears within a dream that can be said to be not actually present. In most dream systems, this will encompass everything within a dream and is the basis on which the LIF® rests. However, I do not deny the possibility that real entities (spirits, deities, etc.) may sometimes enter dreams or dream-like states. In my experience, encountering such 'real' presences feels very different to symbolic people in an ordinary dream. This is difficult to communicate to those who have not experienced this phenomena, but it is worth keeping an open mind when interpreting for others.

Dreams (book): *Dreams* by Carl Gustav Jung contains his most important writings about dream interpretation. For a thorough grounding in Jung's approach to interpretation, this is essential reading.

Dreamscape: The Dreamscape is to dreams what the landscape is to waking consciousness. In the LIF®, it encompasses the dream landscape, Directionology, the elements and buildings, including individual rooms. The Dreamscape forms the background against which the 'actors' in the dream, which include people, animals, plants and objects, 'perform'.

Ego: One of three psychological structures posited by Freud in his structural model of the psyche. The ego mediates between the impulses of the id and the learned rules of the super-ego, driving the personality like a rider controlling a horse.

Esoteric: Something which is aimed at and likely to be understood by a select few.

Felt sense: Defined by Eugene Gendlin, the felt sense is a hard to describe sensation of 'bodily awareness' which communicates inner knowing to the conscious mind. The felt sense is important in Gendlin's 'focusing' technique. In the LIF®, the felt sense is used to confirm that a dream interpretation is on the right track.

Feng shui: A Chinese belief system which has the goal of bringing people into harmony with their environment. Feng shui is based upon the flow of an invisible force known as qi which can be beneficial or harmful to humans depending on factors in their living space and the wider environment. The art of feng shui is in organising space to maximise the beneficial aspects of qi leading to health, wealth and happiness.

Focusing: A technique invented by psychotherapist Eugene Gendlin of the University of Chicago. Gendlin studied successful and unsuccessful cases of psychotherapeutic intervention and concluded that patients who attended to their vague feelings of bodily awareness (which he termed the 'felt sense') were more likely to improve. Gendlin promoted focusing to help people in all situations recognise and make use of the felt sense in self-healing.

Freud, Sigmund: Born in Austria, neurologist Sigmund Freud became one of the most famous names in psychology after he founded the field of psychoanalysis. This novel approach involved treating psychological disorders through dialogue between the psychoanalyst and patient. Among Freud's formulations was the idea that dreams were wish-fulfillments born from unconscious 'repressed' drives and the censor's attempt to disguise the latent dream using displacement, condensation and other techniques. Freud believed that analysing dreams provided a way to access the unconscious and find the root of neuroses. Freud is also known for using the technique of free association, for the concept of the Oedipus complex and for the regulating construct he termed the ego.

Gendlin, Eugene: An American philosopher and psychologist best known for his invention of the technique of focusing. Focusing includes developing awareness of a bodily form of knowing Gendlin termed the felt sense. The felt sense is used in the LIF® as a way of confirming or denying the validity of an ongoing interpretation.

Hall, Calvin S.: Calvin Springer Hall was an American psychologist best known for his extensive dream interpretation work. Hall had over 50,000 dream reports in his possession at the time of his death in 1985.

Harner, Michael: An anthropologist who is credited with the creation of core shamanism, a system of spiritual practice based on traditional forms of shamanism but suitable for the modern age. His book *Way of the Shaman* is a classic in the field.

Howe Jr., Elias: An inventor who advanced the concept of the sewing machine. One of his inventions was the placing of the needle's eye next to the point. He credited this breakthrough to a dream.

Howlite: A crystal used in dream incubation for improving dream recall. It consists of calcium borosilicate hydroxide and is white or transparent in colour.

Integration: The main work in Jungian psychotherapy. Integration is the psychological acceptance of various components of the psyche, starting with the shadow and moving on to the anima/animus.

Journeys out of the Body (book): Robert Monroe's classic detailing his experiences regarding out of body experiences (OOBEs). It contains a biographical account of the development of his abilities and includes instructions on how to achieve an OOBE.

Jung, Carl Gustav: An influential psychiatrist who founded the field of analytical psychology. He was initially a protege of Freud's but the pair diverged on their ideas about the reality of the human psyche. Jung's book *Dreams* presents all of his major work in this area.

Kekule, Friedrich: Friedrich August Kekele was a 19th Century organic chemist who founded the theory of chemical structure. Kekule was a prolific dreamer and first realised that benzene formed a ring when he dreamt of a snake eating its tail - the classic ourobouros symbol.

Kenhirkhopeshef: A scribe who lived around 1,000 years ago in Egypt. He died in possession of an old book of dream interpretation and was one of the first known practitioners of oneirology.

Kleitman, Nathaniel: The father of modern dream research, Kleitman and his students Eugene Aserinsky and William C. Dement pioneered the scientific study of sleep. Working from the University of Chicago, Kleitman and his students were the first to discover REM sleep and associate it with dreaming.

Latent Dream: In his psychoanalytic theory, Sigmund Freud split dreams into two parts. The latent dream resides in the unconscious and consists of various tendencies. The censor, a force acting to ensure unwanted tendencies remain unconscious, modifies the latent dream via the condensation and displacement of dream symbols. The resultant conscious dream Freud termed the manifest dream.

Let Your Body Interpret Your Dreams (book): Author Eugene Gendlin applies his concept of the 'felt sense', taken from his technique of focusing, to dream interpretation. Gendlin stated that interpretation is validated within the body or not at all. Following Gendlin's approach allows those using the LIF® to combine an objective, analytical system with the dreamer's own subjectivity. A truly holistic interpretative system.

LIF® (Layered Interpretative Framework): A unique dream interpretation framework that approaches each dream in a structured way based on layers of dream symbolism. Combined with the use of the 'felt sense' borrowed from the ideas of Eugene Gendlin, the LIF® can be used to interpret any dream.

Loewi, Otto: Born in Germany in the late 19th century, Otto Loewi was a pharmacologist and psychobiologist. He is credited with the discovery of acetylcholine. His theories about the existence of chemical neurotransmitters werenproven with the help of dreamwork.

Lucid Dreaming: A type of experience in which a person 'wakes up' during a dream. There are various degrees of lucid dreaming, from a vague awareness of being inside a dream to complete control over a dream's content. Lab experiments have confirmed that subjects experiencing lucid dreams can sometimes communicate with researchers using eye movements.

Manifest Dream: In his psychoanalytic theory, Sigmund Freud split dreams into two parts. The latent dream resides in the unconscious and consists of various tendencies. The censor, a force acting to ensure unwanted tendencies remain unconscious, modifies the latent dream via the condensation and displacement of dream symbols. Freud termed the resultant conscious dream the manifest dream.

McCartney, Sir Paul: A songwriter for hit 60s pop band, *The Beatles*, Sir Paul McCartney dreamed the melody of one of the band's greatest hits: *Yesterday.*

Melatonin: A hormone produced by the pineal gland. It helps to regulate sleeping and waking in humans and other animals.

Monroe Institute: The Monroe Insttitute (TMI) is a research facility in Virginia dedicated to the exploration of human consciousness. It was founded by Robert Monroe following his out of body experiences (OOBEs).

Monroe, Robert: A radio executive who spontaneously started having out f body experiences (OOBEs). He subsequently founded The Monroe Institute (TMI).

Mythologems: The fundamental patterns that make up the core of human myths and stories. To Jung, mythologems were to myths what the archetypes were to powerful individual expriences and dreams.

Mythology: The study of myths and legends. This can inform dream research since, according to Jung, the same archetypes which are at work in powerful dreams are at the core of our collective folklore.

Nebuchadnezzar: The king of Babylon in around 600 B.C. He is said to have captured Daniel the Hebrew and trained him in magic, which included the interpretation of dreams.

New Age: A loose term encompassing various belief systems, philosophies and practices characterised by a spiritual approach to life. Many New Age systems incorporate astrology and believe humanity are presently entering - or are about to enter - the Age of Aquarius, an era of spiritual enlightenment.

Nightmare: A particularly frightening or shocking dream. My experiences suggest that the nightmare is sometimes used by the Dream Source to force the dreamer to pay attention to a dream and to talk about it with others.

Niklaus, Jack: One of the greatest golfers of all time, Niklaus used dreamwork to improve his swing.

Non-ordinary Reality: A shamanic concept based on belief in an alternative dimension of existence/consciousness which coincides with the mundane existence/consciousness we usually experience. Non-ordinary reality is believed to be just as real as ordinary reality but with its own natural laws. Within this realm, shamans travel through familiar or fantastic landscapes and contact spirits, including the spirit forms of animals, plants and non-organic forms.

Entering non-ordinary reality requires the shaman to alter their consciousness using drumming, psychotropic drugs, chanting and other methods.

Occult: Translated as 'hidden', the term occult is often attached to beliefs, practices and materials which are not available to, or understood by, the general public. Occult matters often have sinister connotations.

Oneirology: The study and interpretation of dreams.

OOBEs: Out of body experiences. A type of experience in which the subject feels they have left their physical body behind. OOBEs are usually spontaneous but can sometimes be planned. They may involve the experience of flight, rapid travel and passing through solid objects. The near death experience (NDE) is a special type of OOBE which occurs when a subject is on the verge of death (e.g., following an accident or during an operation). NDEs often include the experience of a tunnel, a bright light, feelings of peace and wellbeing and an instruction, often from departed loved ones, to return to the physical body.

Ourobouros: A common dream symbol which features a snake eating its own tail.

Pharaoh: A monarch of Ancient Egypt. The Pharaohs were seen as intermediaries between the gods and the people.

Philosophy: The study of thought and the origins of knowledge.

Power Animal: In shamanic belief systems, power animals or totems are seen as both independent spiritual entities and an instinctive part of human nature. Journeying into non-ordinary reality to meet one's power animals is believed to enable the individual to access inner abilities and healing.

Projection: In psychoanalytic theory, people deal with unpalatable aspects of their own psyche by perceiving them as coming from others. This is termed projection. As these aspects are often repressed by the ego (locked into the unconscious), the client is unusually aware of the process. An example is someone who is outwardly calm but is repressing a lot of anger. They may see other people asnhostile due tc the projection of their own unwanted angry impulses.

Psyche: The totality of the mind, including both conscious and unconscious processes. In some belief systems, and commonly in the past, psyche is synonymous with the soul.

Psychiatrist: A doctor who specialises in treating patients with mental health disorders.

Psychoanalysis: A set of psychological theories and associated techniques for treating certain mental health problems.

Psychodynamics: A field of psychology with studies conscious and unconscious forces, and their interplay, in the human psyche.

Psychologist: A professional who studies mental processes and behaviours, usually in humans.

Psychopomp: In shamanism and certain religions, a psychopomp is a human or non-human spirit or soul which acts as a guide to the souls of the deceased, helping them to safely navigate non-ordinary reality. A psychopomp in Jungian psychology mediates between the conscious and unconscious and may take the form of a wise human or animal.

REM Sleep: Rapid eye movement (REM) sleep is, as the name suggests, characterised by small, rapid eye movements. The pioneering work of Kleitman and his students, Aserinsky and Dement, in Chicago, proved that REM sleep was linked to the experience of dreaming.

Repression: In psychoanalytic theory, repression is the result of the ego's refusal to allow unconscious forces into conscious awareness. According to psychoanalysts, repressed psychodynamic forces are expressed through language and behaviours. Psychoanalysis is used in therapy to interpret such language and behaviours.

Secondary Elaboration: A process by which the ego adjusts the form and recall of a latent dream to make the manifest dream more comfortable for the dreamer. It may involve the alteration of dream symbols and the omission of certain details.

Shadow: The shadow is the part of the individual psyche that contains everything we consciously deny in ourselves. It is also the name given to one of the Jungian archetypes and, at its deepest layers, the shadow merges with the collecive unconscious. Integration of the shadow is the first step in analytical psychology and is the precursor to integrating the anima/animus. The less aware we are of our shadow, the more likely it is that we will project these hidden aspects of our psyche onto other people and groups. In dreams, the shadow comes in many guises and is often, though not always, perceived as frightening or threatening.

Shaman: A practitioner of shamanism, an ancient belief system which is still adhered to by indigenous tribes in some parts of the world. A form of modern shamanism, termed 'core shamanism', is popular in Western countries.

Shamanic Journey: An experience within non-ordinary reality which can be spontaneous or planned. Shamanic journeys are usually embarked upon to bring healing power or guidance to the self or others.

Shelley, Mary: A 19th century novelist famous for creating the Gothic novel ***Frankenstein*** (or ***The Modern Prometheus***). The monster from the novel was originally conceived during a dream, or daydream, while Shelley was staying at the home of Lord Byron.

Subconscious: A term often used to describe an area of the psyche which is partly conscious and partly unconscious. Although Freud did use the term in his early work, he later rejected it in favour of a binary conscious/unconscious model.

The Interpretation of Dreams (book): Freud's 1899 book which laid out his theories on the unconscious and how it affects dreams. The Oedipus complex is also introduced in this work.

Theosophical Society: A society founded on Theosophy, a belief system which claims that spiritual knowledge and wisdom can, and should, be obtained directly by truth-seekers rather than through religious interpreters. The Theosophical Society was formed in 1875 by HP Blavatsky and others.

Walker, Madam C.J.: Born Sarah Breedlove, Madame C.J. Walker was the first female self-made millionaire in America and became one of the wealthiest African American women in the country. Madam Walker made her fortune in the hair and beauty market and received assistance from her dreams in developing the formula for combating alopecia (male pattern baldness).

Way of the Shaman (book): Michael Harner's classic book which provides both a fascinating insight into the shamanistic practices of indigenous South American cultures and a guidebook to 'core shamanism,' A significant contribution to Western spiritual experience in the 21st Century.

Wicca/Witchcraft: Witchcraft is an umbrella term for various nature-based spiritual and religious practices with their roots in ancient history. Wicca is a modern formulation of the principles of witchcraft.

Wish-fulfilment: In psychoanalytic theory, wish-fulfilment is the psychological satisfaction of a desire. This may come about through dreaming and, according to psychoanalysts, is often disguised and requires interpretation.

ABOUT THE DREAM GUY

Neil (aka The Dream Guy) is a non-fiction and fiction writer with a background in dream interpretation, astrology and cartomancy.

He set up nhBeyond as a platform for exploring topics outside of mainstream conversation, including philosophy, religion, quantum physics, spirituality, shamanism, divination, astral projection, UFO/UAPs, cryptozoology, the occult and witchcraft.

With a BSc(Hons) degree in psychology, Neil balances his scientific training with an open-minded attitude to life and the Universe. This comes from his family background and personal experiences.

For more information: https://nhbeyond.com

www.ingramcontent.com/pod-product-compliance
Lightning Source LLC
LaVergne TN
LVHW020030170826
845678LV00001B/204

* 9 7 8 1 3 9 9 9 8 4 4 3 0 *